D1719583

Theatre Research Resources
in
New York City

Sixth Edition
2007

Edited by Jessica Brater

Originally compiled by
Philip Alexander and David Underwood

Previously revised and updated by
Joshua Abrams, Abraham Marcus,
Marion Wilson, and Amy Hughes

Marvin Carlson, Senior Editor

Martin E. Segal Theatre Center
Daniel Gerould, Executive Director
Frank Hentschker, Director of Programs
Jan Stenzel, Director of Administration

THE LIBRARY OF CONGRESS HAS CATALOGED THE FIFTH EDITION AS FOLLOWS:

Theatre research resources in New York City / Senior editor, Marvin Carlson ; edited by Amy Hughes ; originally compiled by Philip Alexander and David Underwood ; revised and updated by Joshua Abrams ... [et al.].
    p. cm.
    Includes index.
    ISBN 0-9666152-7-1 (alk. paper)
    1. Theater--Archival resources--Directories. 2. Theater--Library resources--Directories. 3. Archival resources--New York (State)--New York--Directories. 4. Library resources--New York (State)--New York--Directories. I. Carlson, Marvin A., 1935- II. Hughes, Amy. III. Alexander, Philip

PN2289.T545 2004
026.792'025'025'7471--dc22

                         20040524422

Sixth Edition ISBN: 978-0-9790570-0-7

On the cover: Architectural rendering circa 1933 of the Helen Hayes Theatre, 210 West 46th Street, New York City, designed by Herts and Tallant (no longer extant). Courtesy of The Library of Congress, Prints and Photographs Division, Historic American Buildings Survey, HABS,NY,31-NEYO,84.

Contents

Editor's Note

This guide to theatre research resources in New York City is based upon interviews with archivists, current printed guides to collections, and information provided by the collections on the Internet. We have made it as accurate and complete as possible. Nevertheless, the subject is so large that omissions and errors may have occurred. We would greatly appreciate any additions or corrections for future printings. Please send them to mestc@gc.cuny.edu or to The Martin E. Segal Theatre Center, 365 Fifth Avenue, 3rd Floor, New York, NY 10016.

Although we are not able to list databases, we should like to call your attention to The Lortel Archives. Also known as www.IOBDB.com (Internet Off-Broadway Database), the Lortel Archives provides a catalogue of all Off-Broadway shows that have played at a Manhattan theatre with a seating capacity of 100-499 and were intended to run for a closed-ended or open-ended schedule of performances of more than one week for both critics and general audiences.
Website: www.lortel.org/LLA_archive/index.cfm

Researchers wishing to use any special collection are urged to contact the archivist or librarian in advance, both as a courtesy to the archive and as a guarantee of the most efficient use of research time. Public and college libraries in New York are normally open to researchers by means of a special temporary permit, the Library Metro Card, issued by the libraries.

We wish to thank the many archivists and librarians who assisted us in this compilation. These editions have also benefited from the thoughtful attention of Frank Hentschker, Jan Stenzel, Kimon Keramidas, Jill Stevenson and Amy Hughes.

Actors Studio

Archive not open to the public.

American Academy of Arts and Letters

633 West 155th Street
New York, NY 10032
(212) 386-5900
Fax: (212) 491-4615
www.artsandletters.org

Jane Bolster, Librarian
Kathy Kienholz, Archivist

Hours: 9:30 am – 5:00 pm, Monday to Friday

Holdings: Letters and memorabilia related to members of the academy, including some manuscripts and clippings. Past and present members include Stephen Sondheim, John Guare, and J. M. Barrie.

American Academy of Dramatic Arts

120 Madison Avenue
New York, NY 10016
(212) 686-9244, ext. 337
Fax: (212) 685-8093
www.aada.org

Deborah Picone, Head Librarian

Hours: 10:00 am – 6:00pm, Monday to Friday

Holdings: Described as an actors' library, the collection is designed to provide historical and cultural background for production, especially of Russian, Irish, and English plays. Non-book materials include 600 documentary videotapes and 250 audio and dialect tapes. Reference materials also include materials related to the performance of *commedia dell'arte*, Restoration drama, and classical Greek plays.

Special Services: A library Metro Card is required and an appointment must be made 24 hours in advance.

American Irish Historical Society

991 Fifth Avenue
New York, NY 10028
(212) 288-2263
Fax: (212) 628-7927
www.aihs.org
research@aihs.org

Hours: 10:30 am – 5:00 pm, Monday to Friday, by appointment only

Subject Strengths: Irish history and literature; emphasis on the Irish immigrant's experience and contribution to the development of American society; little related directly to theatre.

Holdings: 10,000+ volumes. Large periodical collection and newspapers published in the U.S.

Special Collections: Irish Text Society editions (100+ dual language volumes); editions of texts in Middle Irish; facsimiles of Irish MSS, several organizations' and individuals' papers and works. Popular Culture Collection.

Services: Collections are open for on-site research; those planning to use the collection should call for an appointment. Membership entitles a researcher to browse the stacks.

American Jewish Committee

Human Relations Research Library

Jacob Blaustein Building
165 East 56th Street
New York, NY 10022
(212) 751-4000
Fax: (212) 838-2120
www.ajc.org
library@ajc.org

Cyma Horowitz, Librarian

Hours: 9:30 am – 5:30 pm, Monday to Friday

Holdings: Although primarily concerned with contemporary American Jewish issues, the library features a comprehensive collection addressing Jewish communities worldwide. The library houses 250 current periodical titles, 25,000 volumes, and 30 vertical files.

Oral History Library

Dorot Jewish Division
NYPL Humanities and Social Sciences Library
42nd Street and Fifth Avenue
(212) 930-0601
Fax (212) 642-0141
www.nypl.org/research/chss/jws/oralhistories2.cfm
freidus@nypl.org

Michael Terry, Dorot Chief Librarian

Hours: 11:00 am – 7:30 pm, Tuesday and Wednesday
10:00 am – 6:00 pm, Thursday to Saturday

Subject Strengths: Gathered over a period of 20 years, the collection chronicles the lives of more than 2,000 memoirists with varying backgrounds. Housed at the New York Public Library's Dorot Jewish Division, the special collections section includes oral histories of approximately 70 people associated with Yiddish theatre in America.

Services: This resource is described in the four volumes of the *Catalogue of Memoirs of the William E. Weiner Oral History Library*. Memoirs, unless restricted, are made available to qualified researchers by appointment.

AMERICAN MUSEUM OF NATURAL HISTORY LIBRARY

79th Street and Central Park West
New York, NY 10024
(212) 769-5400
Fax: (212) 769-5009
library.amnh.org
libref@amnh.org

Tom Baione, Senior Librarian for Client Services

Hours: 2:00 pm – 5:30 pm, Tuesday, Wednesday, Thursday

Holdings: In addition to covering various topics in natural history, the Library collects works in anthropology, which may include research on performances and rituals in indigenous societies. The collection is rich in historical materials.

Services: The library is open to the public; copying is available.

AMERICAN PLACE THEATRE

266 West 37th Street, 22nd Floor
New York, NY 10018
(212) 594-4482
Fax: (212) 594-4208
www.americanplacetheatre.org
contact@americanplacetheatre.org

David Kener, Executive Director

Holdings: The archives contain materials related to productions since 1964, including production books, clippings, and reviews. Call for an appointment.

AMERICAN THEATRE WING

Private theatre collection is not open for research.

AMERICAS SOCIETY

680 Park Avenue (at 68th Street)
New York, NY 10021
(212) 249-8950
Fax: (212) 249-5868
www.americas-society.org/as
gmartin@as-coa.org

Marysol Nieves, Director of Visual Arts

Hours: Monday to Friday, by appointment only

Subject Strengths: The library's strength is its collection of over 5,000 fine art books documenting the history of art in the Americas (Canada, the Caribbean, and Latin America) from pre-Columbian and colonial to modern and contemporary art. Exhibition catalogues and slides document the history of the society's exhibition program.

Services: Most items are not catalogued. Requests for appointments should be submitted in writing at least one week prior to the desired date.

ANTHOLOGY FILM ARCHIVES

32 Second Avenue
New York, NY 10003
(212) 505-5181
Fax: (212) 477-2714
www.anthologyfilmarchives.org

Andrew Lampert, Film Archivist
andrew@anthologyfilmarchives.org

Robert Haller
Director of Collection/Special Projects
dev@anthologyfilmarchives.org

Hours: By appointment only.

Subject Strengths: Although the collection focuses on the collection of materials related to avant-garde and independent films and filmmakers, it does not lack resources related to mainstream film and experimental theater. In particular, collections have been established for Maya Derren, David Brooks, Jerome Hill, Joseph Cornell, Marie Menken, Paul Sharits, Barbara Rubin, Christopher Maclaine, Ron Rice, Bob Fleischner, and others.

Holdings: 10,000 books; 11,000 clipping files; 1,000 photo files; 280 series of periodicals, many spanning 20-30 years; a 60,000 bibliographic card index of filmmakers.

Services: Films in the collection may be viewed in the research center. Fees for viewing range from $30 to $100 per hour, depending on format. Xeroxing of non-copyrighted materials is available. Appointments should be arranged at least one week in advance.

ARMSTEAD-JOHNSON FOUNDATION FOR THEATRE RESEARCH

Collection materials and administrative papers are now housed at The Schomburg Center for Research in Black Culture (see entry under New York Public Library).

LOUIS ARMSTRONG HOUSE AND ARCHIVE

Benjamin Rosenthal Library, Queens College
65-30 Kissena Boulevard
Flushing, NY 11367
(718) 997-3670
Fax: (718) 997-3677
www.louisarmstronghouse.org
info@louisarmstronghouse.org

Michael Cogswell, Director

Hours: By appointment only.

Subject Strengths: The archive is the repository of all the personal papers, manuscript music, sound recordings, scrapbooks, photographs, awards and other materials from Louis Armstrong's personal collection.

Holdings: Reel-to-reel tapes; 78s, LPs, 45s; scrapbooks; photographs; manuscript band parts; personal papers; books and journals; trumpets and mouthpieces; awards.

AUSTRIAN CULTURAL FORUM

11 East 52nd Street
New York, NY 10022
(212) 319-5300, ext. 208
Fax: (212) 644-8660
www.acfny.org

Manfred Kapper, Librarian
mkapper@acfny.org

Hours: 8:00 am – 4:00 pm, Monday to Friday, by appointment

Subject Strengths: Austrian art, architecture, literature, music, film, and theatre.

Special Collections: Works of the *Minnesaenger*; facsimiles of medieval manuscripts (including books of hours); Kindermann's *Theatergeschichte Europas*; books on Austrian theatre structures and festivals; biographies of Austrian theatre artists (some in English); collected editions of many Austrian writers. The ACF maintains a collection of 200+ documentary and feature films and videos on Austrian topics such as Fine Art/Architecture/Design, Music, Literature/Theater, Artists' Biographies, History,

Science/Technology, and The Country/People/Folklore/Sports.

Holdings: 10,000 volumes and 22 periodicals; all holdings are inventoried and catalogued. A description of the medieval holdings of the Austrian Cultural Forum Library is available in the Pearl Kibre Medieval Study at the CUNY Graduate School and University Center.

Services: Collection is open to the public for reference only. Films and videos are available on a free loan basis to educational institutions for non-commercial showings. Additional films, including experimental and avant-garde films by Austrian cinematographers, are available from Austria on request (borrower pays return shipping costs).

LEO BAECK INSTITUTE

15 West 16th Street
New York, NY 10011
(212) 744-6400
Fax: (212) 988-1305
www.lbi.org
lbaeck@lbi.cjh.org

Renate Evers, Head Librarian

Hours: 9:30 am – 4:30 pm, Monday to Thursday, by appointment

Subject Strengths: Information and documentation regarding German-speaking Jews, including emigration. Performance subjects are limited to 19th-century dance, Russian ballet dancers, and ghetto art, which may include theatre in Therezinstadt.

Services: The collection is open for on-site research; those planning to use the collection should call or email for an appointment.

BROOKLYN ACADEMY OF MUSIC

30 Lafayette Avenue
Brooklyn, NY 11217
(718) 636-4111 (Administration)
(718) 638-6559 (Archives)
Fax: (212) 857-2021
www.bam.org

Sharon Lehner, Archivist
slehner@bam.org

Hours: 9:00 am - 5:00 pm, Monday to Friday

Holdings: The archives house correspondence, memoranda, financial and legal papers, programs, annual reports, newsletters, magazines, pamphlets, bulletins, prospecti, journals, posters, promotional materials, and other items related to presentations at BAM, which is the oldest continually operating performing arts institution in the nation. The collection also includes art work, photographs, negatives, slides, newspaper clippings, and video and audio recordings. The bulk of materials is from the last thirty years, with a particular focus on the annual Next Wave Festival, one of the foremost festivals of international contemporary performance. Some items date to BAM's founding in 1858, although most 19th-century materials were destroyed in a 1903 fire.

Services: The very limited operating hours of the archives require that research appointments be made approximately two weeks in advance. Videos of BAM presentations may be viewed at the Theatre on Film and Tape Archive at the NYPL Performing Arts Library, but permission must be secured from BAM in advance—contact the Executive Producer's Office via (212) 636-4111 to make a request.

Brooklyn College (CUNY)

Special Collections Division
2900 Bedford Avenue
Brooklyn, NY 11231-2889
(718) 951-5346
Fax: (718) 951-4557
library.brooklyn.cuny.edu

Anthony M. Cucchiara, Archivist
tonyc@brooklyn.cuny.edu

Hours: 9:00 am – 5:00 pm, Monday to Friday
Evenings by appointment

Subject Strengths: Collections of papers of notable alumni include playwrights and screenwriters, such as Malvin Wald and William Alfred. The collection also houses scrapbooks and set and costume designs, as well as photos and programs of student productions at Brooklyn College, dating from 1932 to the 1980s.

Services: The book titles in the Archives and Special Collections are catalogued and appear in the CUNY+ online catalogue.

Archival materials are catalogued in MICRO-MARC AMC, a special database designed to provide bibliographic control and access to the archival materials. This database is available to researchers in the archives, as are the individual guides prepared for each archival collection. Researchers who are not affiliated with CUNY must make arrangements in advance to access the collection.

BROOKLYN HISTORICAL SOCIETY

128 Pierrepont Street
Brooklyn, NY 11201
(718) 222-4111
Fax: (718) 222-3794

Sean Ashby, Library Assistant
sashby@brooklynhistory.org

Hours: 10:00 am – 5:00 pm, Wednesday, Thursday, Saturday
10:00 am – 8:00 pm, Friday
12:00 pm – 5:00 pm, Sunday

Special Collections: More than 1,000 playbills and programs in MS collection, dated 1722-1911 (also a few play MSS), primarily from Brooklyn, with some items from New York theatres and the Brooklyn Academy of Music (not yet catalogued). The Image Collection features 33,000 images of neighborhoods, streets, landmarks, and the waterfront as well as portraits of residents from the 19th and 20th centuries. There is also an extensive sheet-music collection going as far back as the 19th century.

Services: The library is open for onsite research free of charge to members, $4 to students with ID, and $6 to others.

BROOKLYN MUSEUM LIBRARIES AND ARCHIVES

200 Eastern Parkway
Brooklyn, NY 11238
(718) 638-5000, ext. 307
Fax: (718) 638-3731
www.brooklynmuseum.org
Catalog: http://www.brooklynmuseum.org
library@brooklynmuseum.org

Deidre Lawrence, Principal Librarian

Hours: 1:00 pm - 4:30 pm, Wednesday to Friday, by appointment only

Subject Strengths: Research collections held in two Libraries and an Archive are available primarily for the Museum staff and are open by appointment to advanced researchers. With over 250,000 volumes, the Libraries and Archives have been developed to support research on the Brooklyn Museum and its collections, this non-circulating Library is particularly strong in the art and cultural history of North and South America, Africa, Asia, Egypt, Islam, and Ancient Middle East. The arts are well represented with research material on all aspects of cultural heritage including costume and textiles. Special Collections include an extensive collection of film and theatrical costume sketches created between 1912 and the early 1950's by key American fashion designers.

Services: The Museum Libraries and Archives are open by appointment for advanced research. Appointments must be made at least 24 hours in advance and must be confirmed by Library staff. To inquire about making an appointment please contact library@brooklynmuseum.org or call (718) 501-6307. Open to interested scholars. Materials do not circulate.

CARNEGIE HALL ARCHIVES

881 Seventh Avenue
New York, NY 10019
(212) 903-9629
Fax: (212) 582-5518
www.carnegiehall.org
archives@carnegiehall.org

Gino Francesconi, Archivist

Hours: 9:30 am – 5:30 pm, Monday to Friday, by appointment

Subject Strengths: The history of Carnegie Hall which includes the construction and renovation history; history of events in the four main performance spaces; tenant history of rentals in the 150 studio/office spaces above the theaters.

Holdings: 2,500 square feet of documents, which include administration files; a nearly - complete set of programs from the inaugural week of concerts in 1891; promotional flyers and posters; photographs; audio and video recordings; architectural drawings; musical manuscripts and autographs; tenant information; paintings and drawings . Also located on the Second Floor of the building is the Rose Museum (Open 11am - 4:30pm daily, admission frce) which includes a history of the Hall and more than 200 photos and objects on display.

Services: Call or email for an appointment.

CIRCLE IN THE SQUARE
1633 Broadway
New York, NY 10019
(212) 307-2700
www.circlesquare.org
circleinthesquare@att.net

Ted Mann, Artistic Director
E. Colin O'Leary, Theatre School Director

Holdings: Archival materials are unorganized. The only materials available for particular productions may consist solely of playbills.

CITY CENTER

Materials related to productions at City Center—including *City Center Encores!*—are housed at the City Center of Music and Drama located at Lincoln Center (70 Lincoln Center Plaza, New York, NY). Call (212) 870-4266 for information.

CITY COLLEGE (CUNY)
Archives and Special Collections
Morris Raphael Cohen Library
North Academic Center, Fifth Floor, Room 301
Convent Avenue at 138th Street
New York, NY 10031
(212) 650-7609
Fax: (212) 650-7604
www.ccny.cuny.edu/library
archives@ccny.cuny.edu

(Ms.) Sydney Van Nort, Archivist

Hours: 9:30 am - 5:30 pm, Monday to Friday

Subject Strengths: Books on costuming, Restoration and 18th-century drama, and early 20th-century British writers.

Services: Librarians welcome visits, but will respond to calls, faxes, and emails. All materials are non-circulating. Patrons may bring laptop computers for note-taking.

COLUMBIA UNIVERSITY
Library Information Office
Butler Library, Room 201
535 West 114th Street
New York, NY 10027
(212) 854-2271
www.columbia.edu/cu/lweb

Hours: 9:00 am – 6:00 pm, Monday, Tuesday, Wednesday, Friday
9:00 am – 8:00 pm, Thursday
12:00 pm – 5:00 pm, Saturday and Sunday

For general information about visitor access to the Columbia Libraries, visit www.columbia.edu/cu/lweb/services/lio/ visitors.html, or email lio@columbia.edu.

Avery Architectural and Fine Arts Library
1172 Amsterdam Avenue
New York, NY 10027
(212) 854-3501
Fax: (212) 854-8904
www.columbia.edu/cu/lweb/indiv/avery/index.html
avery@libraries.cul.columbia.edu

Gerald Beasley, Director

Hours: 9:00 am – 11:00 pm, Monday to Thursday
9:00 am – 9:00 pm, Friday
10:00 am – 7:00 pm, Saturday
12:00 pm – 10:00 pm, Sunday
Hours change during Intersessions and holidays. For full schedule see www.columbia.edu/cu/lweb/indiv/avery/hours/html.

Subject Strengths: Architecture, painting, sculpture, decorative arts, archaeology, historic preservation, city planning, and landscape architecture.

Special Collections: Thomas Lamb's original drawings of theatres, other architectural drawings, and books on theatre design and architecture.

Holdings: 400,000+ volumes, 1,900 journals and serials. Drawings and Archives collection includes 1,000,000 original architectural drawings and manuscripts, mostly from the 19th and 20th centuries (available by appointment only; call 212-854-4110).

Services: A part of the Metro consortium, the library is generally not open to the public; library materials may be consulted only if they are unavailable elsewhere in the New York area. Visitors must present a library Metro Card at the Library Information Office (Butler Library, Room 201, 212-854-7309) in order to obtain a one-day pass to the Avery Library. See www.columbia.edu/cu/lweb/services/lio/access/ for further information about access to the Columbia University Libraries. To see records for a majority of the library's holdings for books and serials, search CLIO, the Columbia online catalogue, at http://www.columbia.edu/cu/lweb/. The *Avery Index to Architectural Periodicals*, an index to periodical articles, is available as an online database at the NYPL; search under the subjects "theatres" or "stage settings "

Oral History Research Office

Butler Library, Room 801
535 West 114th Street
New York, NY 10027
(212) 854-7083
Fax: (212) 854-5378
www.columbia.edu/cu/lweb/indiv/oral
oralhist@libraries.cul.columbia.edu

Mary Marshall Clark, Director

Hours: 9:00 am – 5:00 pm, Monday to Friday

Holdings: Contains over 8,000 taped memoirs, and over 1 million pages of transcription.

Subjects: Stage interviews cover the Group Theatre; the Stanislavsky method; the stock company as training ground; "the road"; new methods of acting and directing; the Actors Studio; changes in business methods; the role of "legitimate" theatre in contemporary life; artistic freedom; comparisons of stage with screen techniques; and the concentration of theatre in New York City. Interviews with actors, directors, and producers begin in 1948. The archive also has a larger collection of film-related interviews that include directors, actors, and producers, as well as radical and experimental filmmakers. Recent additions include interviews with Jerry Schoenfeld and Adolph Green, and a video interview with Judith Malina will be available on the website later this year.

Services: The collection is open to the public (no appointment necessary), and most interviews are available on microfiche. Interviews are catalogued on Research Libraries Information Network (RLIN). First-time visitors should plan to correlate their visit with paging hours at the Rare Book and Manuscript Library (Monday 12:00 pm – 4:00 pm, Tuesday to Friday 9:00 am – 11:45 am and 2:15 pm – 4:00 pm).

Rare Book and Manuscript Library
Butler Library, 6th Floor East
535 West 114th Street
New York, NY 10027
(212) 854-5153
Fax: (212) 854-1365
www.columbia.edu/cu/libraries/indiv/rare
rarebooks@libraries.cul.columbia.edu

Tara C. Craig, Reference Services Supervisor
(212) 854-5590

Hours: 12:00 pm – 7:45 pm, Monday
9:00 am – 4:45 pm, Tuesday to Friday

Holdings: Holdings are listing in the National Union Catalogue of Manuscript Collections—600,000 books, including incunabula; manuscript catalogues; 26 million manuscripts and papers in the entire collection. (Not all materials are listed in CLIO, the library's main catalogue.) In addition, a large number of collections, including some book collections, are now housed offsite. Consult a RBML librarian or visit the division's web page for information.

Special Collections: A recently published catalog, *The Brander Matthews Dramatic Museum*, provides an overview and history of the collection. Theatre-related materials include the papers of

Robert Wilson; a huge collection from the Brander Matthews Dramatic Museum, including books, papers, recordings, puppets, masks, theatre models, admission tokens, and medals; the Sam and Bella Spewack papers; John Daly's theatre records (1872-1899); the Seymour Sym papers (off and off-off-Broadway theatre publicity and clippings, 1955-1994); the Tennessee Williams papers; the L. S. Alexander Gumby Collection of Negroiana; the Joseph Urban papers, with drawings, photographs and set models for a wide variety of productions; the Annie Laurie Williams papers, featuring material relating to stage and film versions of works by authors such as John Steinbeck, John Hersey, and Margaret Mitchell; the Paul Palmer Collection, featuring correspondence and photographs of film and theatre notables from the 1930s through the 1970s. Also numerous collections of medieval manuscripts.

Services: The library is open to qualified researchers; a library Metro Card is required to use the Rare Book collections. An introductory letter from a current professor is required for all undergraduate students. A photo ID is required for entrance to Butler Library.

COOPER-HEWITT NATIONAL DESIGN MUSEUM LIBRARY
2 East 91st Street
New York, NY 10128-9990
(212) 849-8330 (reference)
(212) 849-8376 (Drawing, Prints, and Graphic Design)
Fax: (212) 849-8339
www.sil.si.edu
libmail@si.edu (general inquiries)
d&p@ch.si.edu (Drawings, Prints, and Graphic Design)

Gail S. Davidson, Associate Curator

Library Hours: 9:30 am – 5:30 pm, Monday to Friday

Drawings, Prints, and Graphic Design Dept. Hours:
10:30 am – 12:00 pm, 2:00 pm – 4:00 pm, Tuesday

Subject Strengths: The collection focuses on decorative and ornamental design. Theatre design materials primarily consist of set designs, though some costume and architectural designs can be found. Most pieces are from the late 17th and 18th centuries from France and Italy. Twentieth-century American designs are also included. Also available are prints and books concerning festivals, marionettes, and shadow puppets; circus and ballet posters; and reference works on the various theatre arts (including set design). The Drawings, Prints, and Graphic Design Department contains the papers of Henry Dreyfus and the designers who worked on the interiors for Radio City Music Hall.

Holdings: Publications by museum staff include *Summary Catalogue of Drawings and Prints Designed for Theatre in the Cooper-Hewitt Museum* (1965).

Services: Call at least a day ahead to make an appointment at the library and a week ahead for Drawings, Prints, and Graphics. The automated catalogue SIRIS, which contains approximately 90% of the library's listings, is available on the Smithsonian's web site (URL above).

THE FASHION INSTITUTE OF TECHNOLOGY (SUNY)

Gladys Marcus Library
27th Street at 7th Avenue
E-Building, 5th Floor
New York, NY 10001
(212) 217-5590 (for appointments)
Fax: (212) 217-5268

Professor N. J. Wolfe, Director
Professor Joshua Waller, Head of Special Collections

Hours: 9:00 am – 10:00 pm, Monday to Thursday
9:00 am – 6:30 pm, Friday
12:00 pm – 6:00 pm, Saturday
12:00 pm – 5:00 pm, Sunday

Holdings: The library has an extensive collection of costume history prints but is not a theatre costume history collection. Of special note are original fashion sketches from 1888 to the present and fashion periodicals from 1806 to the present in the Special Collections Department.

Services: A library Metro Card is required to use the collection.

FORDHAM UNIVERSITY

Archives and Special Collections
Rose Hill Campus
Bronx, NY 10458-5151
(718) 817-3560
Fax: (718) 817-5776
www.library.fordham.edu/archives/archive.html

Patrice Kane, Head of Archives and Special Collections
kane@fordham.edu

Hours: 9:00 am – 5:00 pm, Monday to Friday

Subject Strengths: Literature, history, and Jesuit authors.

Services: A library Metro Card is required to use the collection.

FRENCH INSTITUTE ALLIANCE FRANÇAISE

22 East 60th Street
New York, NY 10022-1077
(212) 355-6100, ext. 216
Fax: (212) 935-4119
www.fiaf.org
library@fiaf.org

Hours: 1:30 pm – 8:00 pm, Monday to Thursday
       9:30 am – 3:00 pm, Saturday
       Reference Desk closes at 1:30 pm on Saturday

Subject Strengths: Art, architecture, and civilization of France and French-speaking countries; French language, history, literature, and philosophy; French theatre through the ages including early 20th-century plays often overlooked; biographies and literary criticism.

Special Collections: The Paris Collection (guidebooks, photographs, and historical material relating to the city of Paris); the *Petite Illustration* collection; a good costume collection through the ages and some fashion; contemporary plays being performed in France, but no set designs.

Holdings: 30,000 volumes, 100 periodicals (including *Avant-Scene* theatre magazine), CD-ROMs, audiocassettes, CDs, and videos.

Services: The library is a private collection, primarily for the use of its members, but the reading room is open to the public.

FRICK ART REFERENCE LIBRARY
10 East 71st Street
New York, NY 10021-4967
(212) 547 0641
Fax: (212) 879-2091
http://www.frick.org/library/index.htmreference@frick.org
Email: library@frick.org

Patricia Barnett, Head Librarian

Hours: 10:00 am – 5:00 pm, Monday to Friday
9:30 am – 1:00 pm, Saturday (except June and July)
Closed during August

Subject Strengths: History of Western painting, drawing, sculpture, and illuminated manuscripts from the 5th to the early 20th century. Decorative arts as related to the holdings of The Frick Collection; performing arts as related to the broader study of the fine arts in Europe and the Americas from the 4th to the 20th century.

Special Collections: The Photoarchive includes more than 1 million items, indexed by artist, subject, and collection, including 66,300 photographs of illuminated manuscripts. Extensive collections of microforms and online resources, including the Vatican Cicognara Library; Witt Library photo-archive; Art Sales Online; Avery Index to Architectural Periodical. The Archives contain materials pertaining to The Frick Collection and Frick Art Reference Library; selected archives for scholars and art dealers; materials owned by the Helen Clay Frick Foundation pertaining to the Frick family and its art collecting.

Services: Closed stacks. No material may be requested one hour prior to closing. Copying available. First-time visitors must complete a form to gain access—see the web site for admission policies. The Archives are accessible by appointment only.

Goethe-Institut New York

Library and Information Services
1014 Fifth Avenue
New York, NY 10028
(212) 439-8688
Toll-free (877) GOETHE1
Fax: (212) 439-8705
www.goethe.de/newyork
library@newyork.goethe.org

Marilen Daum, Head Librarian

Hours: 12:00 pm – 7:00 pm, Tuesday and Thursday
12:00 pm – 5:00 pm, Wednesday, Friday, Saturday

Subject Strengths: In addition to copies of German plays, biographies of German performers and directors, and reference books on German performance, Goethe-Institut subscribes to German newspapers and periodicals, including *Theater Heute*.

Holdings: 9,000 volumes in German and in English, 1,000 videos, 85 periodicals, CD collection.

Services: The annual membership fee is $10 ($5 for students). Books, cassettes, videos, or CDs can be borrowed for three weeks. To become a library patron, complete an application and provide current identification.

Solomon R. Guggenheim Museum Library

The archives is currently closed to researchers.

Hampden-Booth Theatre Library (at the Players)

16 Gramercy Park South
New York, NY 10003
(212) 228-1861
Fax: (212) 253-6473
hampdenboo@aol.com

Raymond Wemmlinger, Curator and Librarian

Hours: 9:00 am – 5:00 pm, Monday to Friday

Subject Strengths: The collection is housed in the home of Edward Booth, and concentrates on 19th-century American and British theatre.

Special Collections: The Booth Collection includes prompt-books, correspondence, journals, business records, etc. The Waiter Hampden Collection, the collection of papers from the Union Square Theatre, and the William Henderson Collection of English Playbills (dating from 1747-1888). Smaller collections include the Chuck Callahan Burlesque Collection, the British Actors Orphanage Fund, Franklin Heller promptbooks, the Players Pipe Night Tape Collection, and the papers of such theatre personalities as Maurice Evans, Robert B. Mantell, E. H. Southern, Julia Marlowe, and Charles Coburn. The library's holdings also include stage props and curios of well-known 19th-century actors, and an art collection ranging from painted portraits to death masks.

Services: An appointment may be arranged only after contacting the library and supplying a letter with a list of research topics. Indeces are available.

HATCH-BILLOPS COLLECTION

Archives of Black American Cultural History
491 Broadway, 7th Floor
New York, NY 10012
(212) 966-3231
www.hatch_billopscollection.org

Camille Billops and James Hatch, Founders/Administrators

Hours: By appointment only

Subject Strengths: The collection focuses on visual arts and theatre, though literature, poetry, dance, and film are included in its scope. Holdings related to theatre include books, periodicals, published and unpublished plays, theatre programs from New York City and around the world, posters, oral history tapes, photographs, and clipping files.

Holdings: 10,000 35mm color slides (1973-); 1,500 oral history tapes (1970-); 1,600 exhibition catalogues (1930-); 1,200 theatre programs; 3,000 vertical files; 5,000 photographs; 4,500 books and 1,400 issues of periodicals (1850-).

Special Collections: Owen and Edith Dodson Memorial collection: manuscripts (published and unpublished), theatre programs, play scripts, poems, photographs, correspondence, newspaper reviews, and tape recordings.The 500 plays (1858-) and 450 posters (1920-) formerly housed in the archives have been sent to the Billops Hatch Collection at Emory University.

Services: Call for an appointment. There is a fee of $5 per hour for use of the collection.

HEBREW UNION COLLEGE
Klau Library
Brookdale Center
1 West 4th Street
New York, NY 10012
(212) 674-5300
Fax: (212) 388-1720

Dr. Philip Miller, Head Librarian
pmiller@huc.edu

Hours: 9:00 am – 5:00 pm, Monday to Thursday
9:00 am – 3:00 pm, Friday

Holdings: Primarily a theological library of approximately 130,000 volumes, the collection holds some general works on theatre, including sound recordings and sheet music. Some materials are in Hebrew or Yiddish, but most are in English.

Services: Non-HUC or -NYU students must make advance arrangements in order to access the library.

HISPANIC SOCIETY OF AMERICA
613 West 155th Street
New York, NY 10032
(212) 926-2234
Fax: (212) 690-0743
www.hispanicsociety.org/english
info@hispanicsociety.org

Dr. Gerald MacDonald, Curator, Modern Library
Dr. John O'Neill, Curator, MSS and Rare Books

Hours: 9:00 am – 4:30 pm, Tuesday to Saturday

21

Subject Strengths: Art, history, literature, and general culture of Spain, Portugal, and other Spanish and Portuguese-speaking countries. The collection is in different languages, but about half of the material is in Spanish and Portuguese.

Special Collections: Extensive medieval manuscripts, incunabula, and numismatic collections. A printed catalogue of media titles.

Holdings: 15,000 volumes printed before 1701 (including 260 incunabula); 250,000 volumes and periodicals printed after 1701.

Services: The collection is non-circulating and no material may be photocopied; books may be reserved in advance by telephone. Users must present identification. All requests to study and/or publish manuscripts or other unique material must be approved by the Board of Trustees; written requests are due March 15, June 15, and November 15. (Researchers can view such materials to determine whether they wish to make a formal request.) Manuscripts may be seen only by appointment and only one reader per day may study manuscript material. Reservations must sometimes be made a month or more in advance, since the library can accommodate only three readers of rare books at a time. A catalogue of the printed book collection, *Printed Books 1468-1700 in The Hispanic Society of America* by Clara L. Penney (New York, 1965), is available from the Department of Publications. A supplement to the catalogue is currently in preparation.

INSTITUTO CERVANTES NEW YORK

Biblioteca Jorge Luis Borges
211-215 East 49th Street
New York, NY 10017
(212) 308-7720
Fax: (212) 308-7721
www.cervantes.org
library@cervantes.org

Luis Agusti, Head Librarian
Richard Heyer, Assistant Librarian

Hours: 11:30 am – 7:30 pm, Tuesday and Wednesday
12:00 pm – 7:00 pm, Thursday and Friday
10:00 am – 1:30 pm, Saturday

Subject Strengths: Contemporary Spanish-language authors; literature in Basque, Catalan, and Galician; Spanish authors in English translation; Spanish and Latin-American cinema; comic books; audio books.

Holdings: 70,000 items (books, periodicals, records and audio-tapes, videotapes, slides), 6,000 DVD and videotapes of Spanish and Latin-American movies, documentaries, and TV series.

Services: The reading room is open to the public.

INTERNATIONAL THEATRE INSTITUTE, U.S. CENTER
Theatre Communications Group
520 Eighth Avenue, 24th Floor
New York, NY 10018-5156
(212) 609-5900
Fax: (212) 609-5901
www.tcg.org
iti@tcg.org

Emilya Chachapero, Director

Hours: 12:00 pm – 5:00 pm, Monday to Friday

Subject Strengths: Chartered by UNESCO in 1948 by eleven countries, and now encompassing ninety nations, ITI's resources, accumulated over more than fifty years, focus on contemporary theatre across the globe. Its holdings cover five continents, 106 countries, and ITI's own centers or affiliates. The collection includes many materials from theatres around the world not usually found in this country. A selection of available topics includes Shakespearean production, mime, festivals, puppet theatre, playwrights, directors, cultural exchange, and censorship.

Holdings: 6,100 volumes; over 12,000 playbills; 275 periodicals; and over 12,000 plays from 92 countries, including a significant Theatre of Latin America collection. The library's core is composed of non-book material and theatre ephemera, and includes directories, newsletters, press releases, pamphlets, reviews, and clippings.The "book" portion of the ITI Library [6,100 volumes; over 12,000 playbills; 275 periodicals] has been integrated into the Billy Rose Theatre Collection, available at http://www.nypl.org/research/lpa/the/the.html The non-book portion of the ITI Library [directories, newsletters, press releases, pamphlets, reviews, clippings, and original play manuscripts] is in the midst of being processed and encoded into an archival finding aid. Also included in that archive are the ITI institutional records from 1948-2000.

Services: The Martha W. Coigney/International Theatre Institute Collection was donated to the New York Public Library for the Performing Arts in October 2002. For research queries or access to the collection, contact the NYPL.

ISTITUTO ITALIANO DI CULTURA
686 Park Avenue
New York, NY 10021-5009
(212) 879-4242
Fax: (212) 861-4018
www.italcultny.org
tecno@italcultny.org

Hours: 1:00 pm – 4:30 pm, Monday to Friday

Subject Strengths: Italian language, literature, and related topics. A section on theatre has general theatre books (plays, theatre history) in Italian. An audio-visual department offers films and videos. Current Italian newspapers and clipping files are also available.

Special Collections: Editions of early Italian poetry, poets of the "*dolce stile nuovo*," Dante, Petrarch, and Boccaccio.

Services: Library cards, enabling borrowing privileges, are available to residents of New York, New Jersey, or Connecticut for a $40 annual fee. The catalogue of the library's holdings is available online.

JAPAN SOCIETY
C. V. Starr Library
333 East 47th Street
New York, NY 10017
(212) 832-1155
Fax: (212) 755-6752
www.japansociety.org

Reiko Sassa, Director

Hours: 12:00 pm – 5:00 pm, Monday to Friday

Holdings: 14,000 volumes, primarily in English, on Japanese art, history, culture, society, politics, religion, and many other subjects.

Services: Library open to members and Toyota Language Center students only.

JOYCE THEATRE
175 Eighth Avenue
New York, NY 10019
(212) 691-9740
www.joyce.org
staff@joyce.org

Hours: By appointment only

Holdings: Materials include past playbills and copies of reviews, dating from 1986. Researchers must have specific research topics and call to make an appointment.

THE JUILLIARD SCHOOL
Lila Acheson Wallace Library and Archives
60 Lincoln Center Plaza
New York, NY 10023-6588
(212) 799-5000, ext. 265
Fax: (212) 769-6421
www.juilliard.edu/libraryarchives/libraryarchives.html
library@juilliard.edu

Jane Gottlieb, Vice President for Library and Information Resources

Hours: 8:30 am – 9:00 pm, Monday to Thursday
8:30 am – 7:00 pm, Friday
9:00 am – 5:00 pm, Saturday
1:00 pm – 7:00 pm, Sunday

Special Collections: Holograph scores and letters, rare libretto collection, and archival recordings and videos of Juilliard School Performances.

Holdings: The library includes more than 68,000 scores; 20,000 books on music, dance, drama, and general academic subjects; 25,000 sound recordings; and 1,000 videotapes.

Services: Outside researchers must make appointments and can view only unique materials. Archival holdings are described on the Juilliard web site.

THE KITCHEN

512 West 19th Street
New York, NY 10011
(212) 255-5793, ext. 27
Fax: (212) 645-4258
www.thekitchen.org

Stephen Vitiello, Archivist
stephen@thekitchen.org

Hours: 10:00 am – 6:00 pm, Monday to Friday, by appointment only

Holdings: The archive documents performances at The Kitchen since the 1970s, including early and/or seminal work by artists such as John Cage, Laurie Anderson, Meredith Monk, Bill T. Jones, and others. In addition to programs, clippings, and photographs, the archive includes 3,600 videotapes and 500 audiotapes.

Services: There is a very limited access in-house video-viewing and listening room. Research is by appointment only.

LA MAMA E.T.C.

74A East 4th Street
New York, NY 10003
(212) 260-0579
www.lamama.org
archives@lamama.org

Hours: By appointment only

Subject Strengths: Off-Off-Broadway since 1962. Collection houses scripts, photos, clippings, posters, some design sketches, posters, and videos.

Special Collections: Amiri Baraka's work in the 1960s, overseas production of La Mama E.T.C. under the direction of Tom O'Horgan, Andre Serban (under the name of "Great Jones Repertory Company"), and Will Leach.

Holdings: The archive contains chronological playlists, individual production files, troupe files, international tour files, photos, original artworks, and videos of works by La Mama artists.

Services: By appointment only. Please identify your primary area of interest. A chronological listing of productions since La Mama's founding is available through the Archives page of the website.

LINCOLN CENTER, INC. ARCHIVES

70 Lincoln Center Plaza
New York, NY 10023
(212) 875-5571
Fax: (212) 875-5071
www.lincolncenter.org/aboutlc/archive.asp

Judith Johnson, Director of Information Resources
jjohnson@lincolncenter.org

Hours: 10:00 pm – 4:00 pm, by appointment

Holdings: The archives contain information from 1956 to the present regarding the origins and construction of all the buildings and theatres comprising the Lincoln Center complex. Construction records include correspondence, renderings and other architectural drawings, and photographs. The archive also holds over 65 oral history interviews with architects, administrators, board members, artists, and others concerning the construction and development of Lincoln Center. Another collection is the records of the Lincoln Center Institute, which promotes aesthetic education to teachers and students in the New York City region. These records include correspondence, administrative records, videotapes, and educational packets concerning the varied repertoire of the institute.

MANHATTAN SCHOOL OF MUSIC

The Peter Jay Sharp Library
120 Claremont Avenue
New York, NY 10027
(212) 749-2802, ext. 4511
www.msmnyc.edu/libraries
Catalog: http://library.msmnyc.edu

Peter Caleb, Director of Library Services

Hours: 9:00 am – 9:00 pm, Monday to Thursday
9:00 am – 6:00 pm, Friday
2:00 pm – 8:00 pm, Sunday
Open only to MSM students on Saturday

Holdings: Music books, scores, CDs.

Services: A library Metro Card is required.

MANHATTAN THEATRE CLUB

311 West 43rd Street, 8th Floor
New York, NY 10036
(212) 399-3000
www.manhattantheatreclub.org
questions@mtc-nyc.org

Annie McRae, Play Development Assistant

Holdings: Primarily playbills and scripts. There is a database with information about past productions, allowing for cross-checking and cross-referencing of creative and technical personnel.

MANNES COLLEGE OF MUSIC

Harry Scherman Library
150 West 85th Street
New York, NY 10024
(212) 580-0210, ext. 4803
Fax: (212) 580-1738
library.newschool.edu/scherman

Ed Scarcelle, Library Director
scarcele@newschool.edu

Hours: 8:45 am – 8:45 pm, Monday to Thursday
8:45 am – 4:45 pm, Friday and Saturday
3:45 pm – 7:45 pm, Sunday

Subject Holdings: A music library, its opera holdings include scores, reference books, biographies, opera histories, LPs, CDs, and a collection of over 150 opera videotapes, both of commercial productions and those produced at Mannes.

Services: A library Metro Card is required. Call for an appointment.

METROPOLITAN MUSEUM OF ART

1000 Fifth Avenue (at 82nd Street)
New York, NY 10028
www.metmuseum.org

Department of Drawings and Prints

(212) 570-3920 (prints)
(212) 570-3912 (drawings)

Drue Heinz, Chairman of Drawings
George Goldner, Chairman of Prints

Hours: 10:00 am – 4:30 pm, Tuesday to Friday, by appointment (Closed 12:30 – 2:00 pm)

Subject Strengths: Printed pictures from the 15th century to the present day; illustrated books; drawings for architecture and the decorative arts.

Special Collections: Prints filed under theatre include theatre drawings from several centuries, catalogued by artist. Prints and drawings include work by the Bibblenas, Erte, Ciceri, and Bernocini. An extensive collection of miscellaneous theatre ornaments is listed under "Subject Theatre."

Holdings: 12,000 volumes; 1 million prints and photographs; some incunabula; many 15th-century prints; 10,000 drawings. For information on specific titles, see the published book catalogue, *Library Catalogue of the Metropolitan Museum of Art, New York*, 2nd ed. Boston: G-K Hall, 1980. 48 vols. Supplements 1982-86.

Services: Call in advance for an appointment.

Robert Lehman Collection Library
(212) 650-2340
lehman.library@metmuseum.org

Dr. Laurence Kanter, Curator

Hours: Tuesday to Friday, by appointment only

Subject Strengths: Western European arts of the 13th to the 20th centuries (with special emphasis on the art of Siena); Old Master drawings; Renaissance decorative arts; and studies on illuminated manuscripts.

Holdings: 23,000 volumes and bound periodicals; Robert Lehman collection (letters of connoisseurs and art historians); 5,000 mounted photographs.

Irene Lewisohn Costume Reference Library
(The Costume Institute Library)
(212) 650-2723
Fax: (212) 570-3970
thecostumeinstitute@metmuseum.org

Tatyana Pakhladzhyan, Associate Museum Librarian
Telephone: (212) 396-5233

Hours: 10:00 am – 4:30 pm, Tuesday to Thursday, by appointment only

Subject Strengths: The library possesses a wealth of invaluable information relating to the history of costumes of all countries and periods, and continues acquiring all available books and exhibition catalogs published in the areas of haute couture, fashion, and regional costume.

Special Collections: In January 2004, The Costume Institute Library began a comprehensive reassessment of its archival collections (approximately 750 archival boxes), which contain fashion sketchbooks and sketches, photographs, drawings, prints, post cards, fashion plates, textile swatches, embroidery samples, ephemera, etc. Currently in the process of establishing a thorough inventory of materials with comprehensive computerized documentation, and simultaneously addressing conservation needs for holdings.

Services: The Library is primarily intended for the use of the curatorial staff of The Costume Institute and other Departments of The Metropolitan Museum of Art. In addition, the Library supports the mission of the Museum by serving as a research center for scholars and fashion designers. Outside qualified researchers who have already explored the resources of New York City's other costume research libraries may schedule appointments, subject to staff availability, and preferably arranged three weeks in advance, to use The Costume Institute Library's collection. Prior to their visit, researchers are encouraged to consult the holdings of The Costume Institute Library in WATSONLINE, the Museum libraries' online catalog.

Photograph and Slide Library
(212) 650-2368 (for black-and-white photographs)
(212) 650-2262 (for color transparencies)
(212) 650-2261 (for the slide collection)
Fax: (212) 396-5050

Hours: 10:00 am – 4:30 pm, Tuesday to Friday
Closed in August

Subject Strengths: Art, art history, archaeology, architecture, sculpture, painting, decorative arts.

Holdings: 400,000 slides in 2" x 2" format and 150,000 slides in 3-1/4" x 4" format; black-and-white photographs and large-format transparencies for publication.

Services: Open to the public; identification is necessary to borrow slides.

Thomas J. Watson Library

(212) 650-2225
Fax: (212) 570-3847
watson.library@metmuseum.org

Kenneth Soehner, Chief Librarian

Hours: 10:00 am - 4:40 pm, Tuesday to Friday
Closed last two weeks of August

Subject Strengths: Art, art history, archaeology, painting, sculpture, decorative arts, reflecting the strengths of the museum collections which include objects from all cultures and all time periods; Robert Goldwater Library maintains the collections on the arts of Africa, Oceania, and the Americas.

Special Collections: Art auction/sale catalogues, exhibition catalogues, rare collection catalogues, museum bulletins, early travel books, early trade catalogues, artists' manuals and handbooks, autograph letters, ephemeral files of biographical information on artists, ephemeral material relating to the museum's history.

Holdings: Approximately 600,000 volumes and bound periodicals; 2,500 current periodical subscriptions; microfiche collection; subscriptions to a growing collection of electronic resources.

Services: Open to graduate students and qualified researchers upon presentation of appropriate identification. Reference assistance is available during the hours listed above; consultation in the use of specific electronic resources available by appointment; photocopy service upon request for completion within 48 hours; Central Catalog, which maintains the object records for the museum's collection of more than two million works of art, is open to visitors by appointment, 10:00 am – 1:00 pm, Tuesday to Friday. Call (212) 650-2312 or fax (212) 570-3847. WATSONLINE, the museum libraries' online catalogue, is accessible at http://library.metmuseum.org.

METROPOLITAN OPERA ARCHIVES

Lincoln Center
New York, NY 10023
(212) 799-3100, ext. 2525
Fax: (212) 870-7657
www.metopera.org/history
John Pennino, Assistant Archivist
jpennino@mail.metopera.org

Hours: 9:00 am – 5:00 pm, Monday to Friday, by appointment

Holdings: Memorabilia (programs, photographs, costumes, scenic designs) related to productions dating from 1883 to the present.

Services: An appointment must be arranged in advance, and it is preferred that a letter be sent detailing the needs of the scholar. Collection is open only to those who are writing a book, article, dissertation, or thesis. Graduate students working on term papers are suggested to consult the music collection at the New York Public Performing Arts Library at Lincoln Center.

MORGAN LIBRARY & MUSEUM

29 East 36th Street
New York, NY 10016
(212) 685-0610
Fax: (212) 487-3484
www.morganlibrary.org

Inge Dupont, Head of Reader Services
Rhoda Eitel-Porter, Head of the Drawings and Prints Department

Hours:

> Reading Room: By appointment only
> (212) 590-0315, fax (212) 730-4714
> readingroom@morganlibrary.org

> Drawing Study Center: By appointment only
> (212) 685-0008, ext. 551; fax (212) 685-4740

Holdings: 370,000 rare items. The collections are well known for their illuminated manuscripts, literary and historical manuscripts, early printed books, old master drawings, and music manuscripts.

Special Collections: The Gilbert and Sullivan Collection; The Donald M. Oenslager Collection of Theatre Drawings, containing theatrical, costume, and stage designs, representing works by European, Russian, and American designers, from the 16th to the mid-20th century. The library's online catalogue can be accessed at corsair.morganlibrary.org.

MUSEUM OF CHINESE IN THE AMERICAS
70 Mulberry Street, 2nd Floor
New York, NY 10013
(212) 619-4785
Fax: (212) 619-4720
www.moca-nyc.org
archives@juno.com

Hours: 12:00 pm - 6:00 pm, Tuesday to Sunday, by appointment

Special Collections: Formed primarily from a collection donated by the Chinese Musical and Theatrical Association in New York, the Cantonese Opera Collection includes approximately 190 costumes and accessories, over 160 photographs, 30 hours of oral histories, 100 LPs, a few videotapes and dozens of musical instruments. Paper materials include opera scripts and scores, tickets, pamphlets, announcements, books, and clippings. Materials date from the late 19th century to the present.

Holdings: The library houses 1,000 volumes on Asian-American studies, in addition to documents, photographs, business records, textiles, store signs, and oral histories.

Services: An appointment is required and an application must be completed (available on the web site) for access.

MUSEUM OF MODERN ART (MoMA)
11 West 53 Street, between Fifth and Sixth avenues
New York, NY 10019-5497
(212) 708-9400
www.moma.org

Celeste Bartos Film Study Center
(212) 708-9613 Charles Silver, Associate Curator
(212) 708-9614 Ron Magliozzi, Assistant Curator
Fax: (212) 708-9531
http://www.moma.org/research/studycenters/
Ron_Magliozzi@moma.org (for appointments and questions)

Hours: Monday, Tuesday, Thursday, Friday, by appointment

Subject Strengths: The center has a large collection of screen-plays; extensive clippings files, which include reviews and articles on films and film personalities; posters and pressbooks; and assorted film reference materials and periodicals. Film books and older periodicals are housed in the museum's library. In addition to film holdings, items of theatrical interest include recordings of Sarah Bernhardt, Eleanora Duse, and John Barrymore.

Services: Make arrangements two weeks in advance to view films.

Drawings Study Center
Fax: (212) 708-9556
studycenter_drawings@moma.org

Kathy Curry, Assistant Curator

Hours: 10:00 am – 5:00 pm, by appointment only

Holdings: Most of the museum's 7,000 works on paper, including a special collection of drawings related to the theatre arts, are available to researchers and students through the center. In addition, files and photo albums covering each work in the collection may be consulted. Some of the collection is housed at a second archive site in Queens.

Film Stills Archive
As part of the long-term plan to renovate the museum, the Film Stills Archive has been closed temporarily and moved to The Celeste Bartos Film Preservation Center in Hamlin, PA.

Library
(212) 708-9433
Fax: (212) 333-1122
www.moma.org/research/library
library@moma.org

Hours: 10:00 am – 5:00 pm, Monday, Thursday, Friday, by appointment

Holdings: The museum's library is a comprehensive collection devoted to modern and contemporary art. The non-circulating collection documents painting, sculpture, drawings, prints, photography, architecture, design, performance, video, film, and emerging art forms from 1880 to the present.

Services: Email, fax, or call for an appointment at least one day in advance.

MUSEUM OF TELEVISION AND RADIO
25 West 52nd Street
New York, NY 10019
(212) 621-6713
Fax: (212) 621-6765
www.mtr.org
scholarroom@mtr.org

Hours: 12:00 pm – 6:00 pm, Tuesday to Sunday
12:00 pm – 8:00 pm, Thursday

Subject Holdings: The collection covers more than 70 years of television and radio history from news, public affairs programs, and documentaries, to the performing arts, children's programming, sports, comedy shows, and commercial advertising. The more than 120,000 items include TV and radio programs, divided into two sections: the collection, consisting of readily available material, and the archive, comprising items that are available within 72 hours. Some programs specifically related to theatre are *Uncle Vanya* with Rosemary Harris and Laurence Olivier, *Death of a Salesman* with Dustin Hoffman, and *Hedda Gabler* with Ingrid Berman and Ralph Richardson. Programs are catalogued on computer and available for viewing on 96 monitors.

Services: Adults are suggested to contribute $10 (students $8). Patrons are allowed a maximum of two hours of viewing time. For a $15-25 per diem charge, scholars may use the facility for more than two hours a day, but this must be arranged in advance with a letter to the education department detailing the topic(s) of research. Another option for frequent users is an annual fee of $150 which allows unlimited access to the collection (during operating hours). Applicants should send an email to scholarroom@mtr.org at least two weeks in advance.

MUSEUM OF THE CITY OF NEW YORK
Theatre Collection
1220 Fifth Avenue (enter at 104th Street)
New York, NY 10029
(212) 534-1672, ext. 262
Fax: (212) 534-5974
www.mcny.org
research@mcny.org

Marty Jacobs, Curator

Hours: 9:00 am – 11:30 am, Monday to Friday

Subject Strengths: New York theatre productions, 1866-present (playbills, clippings, photographs), Broadway theatre buildings, silk programs, window cards. The museum houses the private and professional papers of many personalities of the New York stage, including Mary Martin, George M. Cohan, Sophie Tucker, Ethel Merman, and the Barrymore family; holograph scripts by many playwrights, including Eugene O'Neill; the Dazian Library for Theatrical Design (original scene and costume drawings); original designs by Witham, Jones, Oenslager, Aronson, Smith and Lee; and the Yiddish Collection. Publications include exhibition catalogues: Stars of the New York Stage, Musicals of the Thirties, George Gershwin, Biography of a Hit: *Life with Father*, and Broadway Musicals.

Holdings: The collection includes 5,000 stage costumes, thousands of scripts, tens of thousands of photographs, 100 set models, 120,000 programs and 30,000 folders and boxes of materials, each of which is devoted to a separate production or personality.

Services: Call ahead for an appointment one to two weeks in advance. Receipt of an alphabetical list of research topics is requested before the appointment. A $25 per diem research fee ($10 for students) applies for each 2-1/2 hours of research. Photocopies at $.40/page.

NEIGHBORHOOD PLAYHOUSE

340 East 54th Street
New York, NY 10022
(212) 688-3770
Fax: (212) 906-9051
www.neighborhoodplayhouse.org
info@neighborhoodplayhouse.org

David Semonin, Librarian

Hours: 10:30 am – 6:00 pm, Monday to Friday, by appointment only

Subject Strengths: 8,000 reference books, plays, and scores for research for acting students enrolled in the Playhouse's two-year program. Archival material includes papers related to the original playhouse (1915-1927) and photos, promptbooks, and set designs. Materials relating to the school date back to its founding in 1928.

NEW YORK CITY MUNICIPAL ARCHIVES

Department of Records
31 Chambers Street, Room 103
New York, NY 10007
(212) 788-8585
Fax: (212) 788-8583
www.nyc.gov/records (click on the Municipal Archives link)

Leonora Gitlund, Director

Hours: 9:00 am – 4:30 pm, Monday to Thursday
9:00 am – 1:00 pm, Friday

Subject Strengths: As a municipal archive, the collection's focus is on the history of the city government as well as building and legal records. Its efficacy for theatre researchers may be limited.

Special Collections: Real estate assessments (1789-1975), which may include permits for theatres; genealogy and coroner records (1795-1966); court and district attorney records (ca. 1800-1951). Holdings include WPA Federal Writers Project Manuscripts (1936-1943), WNYC Radio and Film Archives (1936-1981), and building permits.

NEW-YORK HISTORICAL SOCIETY LIBRARY

2 West 77th Street
New York, NY 10024
(212) 873-3400
Fax: (212) 875-1591
www.nyhistory.org/library/printroom.html
reference@nyhistory.org

Hours: 10:00 am – 5:00 pm, Tuesday to Saturday
Closed on Saturdays from Memorial Day to Labor Day

Holdings: The society was formed as a repository for American and New York history primarily, but does contain substantial holdings of theatrical value. These include the Emma Thursby Collection of Music and Theatre, and the papers of William Dunlap, Jenny Lind, Baltimore theatrical manager John Thompson Ford, playwright Annie Elizabeth Burke, actor Charles Walter

Couldock, and monologist Ruth Draper. The P. T. Barnum Collection includes a sizeable collection of personal and business materials of the circus entrepreneur. Manuscripts and prompt-books from the 18th and 19th centuries can be found. Holdings concerned with early opera include materials related to Lorenzo Da Ponte and theatre plans. Assorted ephemera such as tickets, posters, programs, and playbills are available, as well as scrap-books from Radio City Music Hall. The society also holds the fourth largest collection of American newspapers published before 1820.

Services: The Prints, Photographs, and Architectural Collection, which contains photos and prints of actors and theatres, is open Tuesday to Friday 10:00 am - 5:00 pm, by appointment only.
Telephone: (212) 873-3400, ext. 227 or 228
Fax: (212) 787-9474
Email: printroom@nyhistory.org

New York Public Library

Note: Patrons requesting materials at NYPL Research Libraries must obtain a special ACCESS card. Visit www.nypl.org/research/general/access.html for information.

Donnell Library Center
20 West 53rd Street
New York, NY 10019
(212) 621-0618
www.nypl.org/branch/central_units/d/donnell.html

Donnell Media Center
(212) 621-0609 (film, video, and sound recordings information)
(212) 621-0610 (reserve collection circulation)
(212) 621-0611 (Study Center appointments)
Fax: (212) 245-5272
www.nypl.org/branch/central_units/d/donnell.html

Joan Byrd, Supervising Librarian
Joe Yranski, Film Video Historian
Elizabeth McMahon, Senior Film Video Librarian

Hours: 10:00 am – 6:00 pm, Monday, Wednesday, Friday
10:00 am – 8:00 pm, Tuesday and Thursday
10:00 am – 5:00 pm, Saturday
1:00 pm – 5:00 pm, Sunday

Special Collections: The spoken word—fiction, poetry, drama, comedy, and documentaries—is a specialty. The collection contains 35,000 music and non-music CDs.

Holdings: Reference materials available include books, periodicals, catalogues, subject lists, evaluations, and study guides. The collection includes over 8,500 16mm films, which circulate free to individuals and non-profits but which are not for classroom use. The collection contains 35,000 3/4" and 1/2" VHS videocassettes that circulate, consisting of original video documentaries, video art, "exemplary" television programs, a few feature films, and instructional videos. The audio division has classical and contemporary folk music on CD. No dialect tapes.

Services: The center provides film information, film and video viewing and circulation, and circulating audio materials. The film information service answers queries on films and videotapes, including documentary, avant-garde, informational and educational and children's films. (In-depth information on theatrical films is available at the library at Lincoln Center.)

Donnell World Languages Collection
(212) 621-0641
Fax: (212) 245-5272
www.nypl.org/branch/central/dlc/df
df@nypl.org

Bosiljka Stevanovic, Department Head

Hours: 10:00 pm – 6:00 pm, Monday, Wednesday, Friday
10:00 am – 8:00 pm, Tuesday
10:00 am – 8:00 pm, Thursday
12:00 pm – 5:00 pm, Saturday
1:00 pm – 5:00 pm, Sunday

Holdings: A circulating library of fiction, non-fiction, and popular books in 80 foreign languages. Countries represented include those in Asia, South America, and Europe, while African countries are minimally represented. In addition to works of literature, poetry, and plays, the library maintains subscriptions to approximately 60 foreign periodicals.

Humanities and Social Sciences Library
Fifth Avenue and 42nd Street
New York, NY 10018
http://www.nypl.org/research/chss/index.html
(212) 930-0830

Art and Architecture Collection
Room 300
(212) 930-0835
Fax: (212) 930-0530
www.nypl.org/research/chss/spe/art/artarc/artarch.html
artref@nypl.org

Clayton Kirking, Chief, Art Information Resources

Hours: 11:00 am – 7:30 pm, Tuesday and Wednesday
10:00 am – 6:00 pm, Thursday and Friday
1:00 pm - 6:00 pm, Satruday

Subjects: Architecture, painting, drawing, sculpture, decorative arts, and related subjects.

Holdings: 405,000 books, serials, and pamphlets; 500,000 clippings (filed by artist); 268 scrapbooks, various subjects. As this is not a theatre collection, it is most useful for its print and online indexes, bibliographies and books on the work of an artist or architect. It does not house design monographs or plans of theatres. "Artists Files on Microfiche" contains ephemeral information on 90,000 artists of all nationalities, working in all media.

Services: Unlike the other Special Collections departments, readers may enter the Art and Architecture Reading Room at any time during the department's hours for public service.

Asian and Middle Eastern Division
Room 219
(212) 930-0616
Fax: (212) 930-0551
www.nypl.org/research/chss/ort/ort.html
asiaref@nypl.org

John M. Lundquist, MLS, PhD, The Susan and Douglas Dillon Chief Librarian of the Asian and Middle Eastern Division

Hours: 11:00 am – 7:30 pm, Tuesday and Wednesday
10:00 am – 6:00 pm, Thursday to Saturday

Subject Strengths: The languages, literature, history, archaeology, and religions of Asia (China, Japan, Tibet, South Asia, Central Asia), the Middle East, and the Ancient East; Islam; Egyptology and Assyriology; history of printing in India.

Holdings: 451,456 volumes; 1,450 serial titles (including newspapers); 6,868 microforms; 1,000 pamphlets. Early periodicals, grammars, encyclopedias, editions, and translations of Asian and Middle Eastern works of literature, including theatre, from the 17th through 19th centuries.

Special Collections: Some theatrical material, much in the original language.

The Berg Collection
Room 320
(212) 930-0802
(212) 930-0803 (questions and general reference inquiries)
Fax: (212) 930-0079
www.nypl.org/research/chss/spe/brg/berg.html
brgref@nypl.org

Isaac Gewirtz, Curator
igewirtz@nypl.org (for questions regarding permissions, loans, and acquisitions)

Hours: 11:00 am - 6:00 pm, Tuesday and Wednesday
10:00 am - 6:00 pm, Thursday to Saturday

Holdings: 30,000 printed items and 2,000 linear feet of manuscripts and archives, including those of George Cram Cook and Susan Glaspell; Gertrude Stein's printed works; the largest manuscript collection of W.B. Yeats outside of Ireland, voluminous Lady Gregory correspondence and manuscripts; typescript and manuscript drafts of Sean O'Casey plays, as well as 24 of his notebooks; typescripts, manuscripts, and galleys of more than a dozen Eugene O'Neill plays; hundreds of letters by George Bernard Shaw; the unpublished and unfinished play *Divorce*, by the Bloomsburyite Vita Sackville-West; and the unpublished play *The Wreck of the Good Ship Benito*, by the Bloomsburyite Dora Carrington.

41

Dorot Jewish Division
Room 84
(212) 930-0601
Fax: (212) 642-0141
www.nypl.org/research/chss/jws/jewish.html
freidus@nypl.org

Michael Terry, Chief Librarian
mterry@nypl.org

Hours: 11:00 am – 7:30 pm, Tuesday and Wednesday
10:00 am – 6:00 pm, Thursday to Saturday

Subject Strengths: Jewish literature, history, and traditionally general works in Hebrew and Yiddish. The Jewish Division shares responsibility with the Billy Rose Theatre Collection at Lincoln Center, and both collections should be consulted to get the greatest coverage of subject matter.

Special Collections: The Boris Thomashefsky Collection includes 300 manuscript plays, role books, and music scores. A collection of Yiddish theatre broadsides. American Yiddish theatre material including numerous scripts. The WPA Theatre Project including Yiddish and Jewish theatre. The regular collection includes plays in Yiddish and Hebrew, plays in English and other languages on Jewish themes. Reference books, biographies, periodicals on the Yiddish theatre. A large collection of Yiddish newspapers and periodicals.

Holdings: 300,000 volumes, periodicals, and microfilms.

Manuscripts and Archives Division
Room 328
(212) 930-0801
www.nypl.org/research/chss/spe/rbk/mss.html
mssref@nypl.org

William Stingone, Curator

Hours: 11:00 am – 5:45 pm, Tuesday and Wednesday
10:00 am – 5:45 pm, Thursday to Saturday

Special Collections: A fairly large number of theatre items, especially on the American theatre, but also European. Includes papers and letters from the following: P. T. Barnum, William De

Mille, Junius Brutus Booth, Jane Cowl, Rosamund Gilder, Lillie Langtree, Otto Brahm, Institoris, various dramatic funds and associations, Anspacher, Minnie Fiske, E. Gordon Craig, Clyde Fitch, The New Theatre League (highlights of the collection include 77 scripts by Bertolt Brecht, Irwin Shaw, and others); outlines of courses taught at the New Theatre School; publications of the New Theatre League; photographs from the Moscow Art Theatre, the WPA Federal Theatre Project, and the Bolshoi Ballet; Otis Skinner; Cornelia Skinner; The Playwrights Production Company Press Department Records 1930s-1960; Barrett A. Clark; drafts of Simonson's *The Stage Is Set* and Gorelik's *New Theatres for Old*; Clurman's columns in *The Nation* (1955-56); Charles Frohman; William Inge; Eugene O'Neill; Lockhart, Sothern, and Marlow. Edward Albee Papers, Drama League of America Papers 1910-1931, John Van Druten Papers. Consult the Dictionary Catalogue of the Manuscript Division for material, most of which was added prior to 1962. Most theatre-related rare books and manuscripts acquired after 1962 are in the Billy Rose Theatre Collection at the NYPL Performing Arts Library.

Services: The collection is for reference only; card of admission required (available at the Special Collections Office, Room 316, which follows the same hours).

Rare Books Division
Room 324
(212) 642-0110
Fax: (212) 302-4815
www.nypl.org/research/chss/spe/rbk/rbooks.html
rbkmss@nypl.org

Stewart Bodner, Acting Curator

Hours: 11:00 am – 5:45 pm, Tuesday and Wednesday
10:00 am – 5:45 pm, Thursday, Friday, Saturday

Special Collections: Notable collection of Shakespeare editions including the "bad" *Hamlet*. Colonial drama and British drama from the period reprinted in the U.S.

Services: The collection is for reference only; card of admission required (available at the Special Collections Office, Room 316). Some materials require 24 hours notice.

Slavic and Baltic Division

Rooms 216-217
(212) 930-0714
Fax: (212) 930-0693
www.nypl.org/research/chss/slv/slav.balt.html
slavicref@nypl.org

Edward Kasinec, Curator

Hours: 11:00 am – 7:30 pm, Tuesday and Wednesday
10:00 am – 6:00 pm, Thursday to Saturday

Subject Strengths: The majority of the collection's materials are in Russian, with Polish, Czech, Slovak, and Ukrainian contributing significant portions to the collection. Other languages found in the division: Serbo-Croation, Bulgarian, Byelorussian, Slovenian, Macedonian, Serbian, Church Slavonic, Lithuanian, Latvian, and Wendic.

Special Collections: Russian holdings include important editions of Turgenev, Dostoevsky, Tolstoi, and Pushkin, as well as first editions of English translations of Turgenev, Chekhov, and Lermontov. In addition to its strong holdings in collected works of dramatists, the Russian collection contains theatrical biographies, histories of theatre, and theatre groups. Stage periodicals include the Soviet publications *Teatr, Teatral'naia Zhizn'* and a run of *Ezhegodnik Imperatorskikh Teatrov* (1890-1919), and 17 plays by Catherine II, which appeared in *Rossiiskii Teatr*, 1786-87. The Hapgood Papers contain letters and photographs, 1888-1922, from Russian writers, artists, religious leaders, etc., including Leo Tolstoi, Maxim Gorky, and Alla Nazimova. The John Jacob Robbins Papers (1883-1953) contain his translations of Pushkin, Lermontov, Blok, Bulgakov, and others as well as correspondence. Included in the papers of Mstislav Dobuzhinsky are a holograph draft of his memoirs, notes and sketches for stage designs for several plays, a history of Russian stage design, a chronology of *Mir Iskusstva*, and an article on Stanislavsky. Ukrainian dramatic literature holdings are minimal and Byelorussian works appear to be primarily periodicals. Collected works of major Latvian authors, together with all standard works in literary criticism of the language, can be found, along with Latvian translations of Dumas, Goethe, and Schiller, and the poetry and drama of Anslvs Eglitis. Polish drama is collected on a representative, rather than a comprehensive, basis. Mickiewicz is represented by 150 entries, with 290 works about him.

Holdings: 450,000+ volumes, 1,200 current serials, and 21,000+ microform titles. In addition, upwards of 300,000 volumes of Slavic and Baltica in Western European languages.

Miriam & Ira D. Wallach Division of Art, Prints, and Photographs
Room 308
(212) 930-0817
Fax: (212) 930-0530
www.nypl.org/research/chss/spe/art/print/print.html
prnref@nypl.org

Roberta Waddell, Curator of Prints

Hours: 1:00 pm – 5:45 pm, Tuesday to Saturday

Subject Strengths: Rare and fine prints of the 15th century to the present; not much theatre. Some reference books depicting theatre and activities related to it. Some material on festivals and processions. See the Spencer Collection catalogue and CATNYP.

Services: Collection is for reference only; card of admission required (available at Special Collections Office, Room 316). It is advisable to request material in advance if you know it is in the collection; Spencer Collection requests require 24 hours advance notice.

Mid-Manhattan Library
455 Fifth Avenue (at 40th Street)
New York, NY 10016
(212) 340-0833
www.nypl.org/branch/central_units/mm/midman.html

Art Collection
Third Floor
(212) 340-0871
www.nypl.org/branch/central_units/mm/art/art.html

Linda Dove, Supervising Librarian

Hours: 9:00 am – 9:00 pm, Monday, Wednesday, Thursday
11:00 am – 7:00 pm, Tuesday
10:00 am – 6:00 pm, Friday and Saturday

Subject Strengths: Fine arts, architecture, graphic art, interior design, landscape architecture, photography.

Holdings: 40,000 volumes; 1,600 bound periodicals; 250 reels of microfilm/fiche; 138 current periodicals; circulating book collection. The collection has little of specific relation to theatre, but offers design work by visual artists and indices for art periodicals.

The Picture Collection
Third Floor
(212) 340-0878
Fax: (212) 576-0048
www.nypl.org/branch/central/mml/pc/index.htm
Online holdings: http://digitalgallery.nypl.org/nypldigital/l
mmpic@nypl.org

David Callahan, Supervising Librarian

Hours: 9:00 am - 9:00 pm, Monday to Wednesday
10:00 am - 6:00 pm, Thursday
10:00 am - 6:00 pm, Friday and Saturday

Holdings: Over 1 million illustrations, photographs, and reproductions of paintings, clipped from books, magazines, and newspapers. The collection also includes a large assortment of postcards and greeting cards. Subject areas include theatre, ancient through present day; theatres (interiors and exteriors); photographs and illustrations of theatrical productions; dance; opera; puppet and puppet theatres; costume and set design; theatre personalities.

Services: Materials may be borrowed for three weeks with a New York Public Library card. A portion of the collection is available over the Internet at picturecollection.nypl.org. Available online holdings can be found at: http://digitalgallery.nypl.org/nypldigital/.

Performing Arts Library

Note: Some materials are housed offsite and require 24 hours notice for retrieval. When a specific title is needed, call (212) 870-1630 to verify availability.

Dorothy and Lewis B. Cullman Center
40 Lincoln Center Plaza
New York, NY 10023
(212) 870-1630
http://www.nypl.org/research/lpa/lpa.html

The Music Division
Third Floor
(212) 870-1650
Fax: (212) 870-1794
www.nypl.org/research/lpa/mus/mus.html
musicdiv@nypl.org

Charles Eubanks, Acting Chief

Hours: 12:00 pm – 6:00 pm, Tuesday, Wednesday, Friday, Saturday
12:00 pm – 8:00 pm, Thursday

Subject Strengths: Chronicling the art of music in all its diversity—opera, chamber orchestral, sacred and secular vocal music, ragtime, jazz, musical comedy, rock, world music and pop music. Particularly noteworthy is the American Music Collection. The collection contains printed books, scores and periodicals, clipping files, programs, photographs, set and costume designs, photos and prints of musicians, autograph letters and signed documents, autograph music manuscripts, and sheet music.

Special Collections: Joseph Drexel Collection (15th-19th century music), Henry Hadley Memorial Library (American composers' scores), Toscanini Memorial Archives (microfilms of music manuscripts), Beethoven Association Collection (books and first editions), Joseph Muller Collection (engravings and lithographs), Otto Hess and William Gottlieb Collections of jazz photographs, Marcella Sembrich Collection, Toscanini Legacy, Burnside Collection (musical theatre manuscripts), and the American Music Center Collection of scores by U.S. composers. Autograph music manuscripts and papers of Henry Cowell, John Cage, Otto Luening, William Schuman, George Rochberg, Vincent Persichetti, Ross Lee Finney, Rosa Ponselle, Rosina Lhevinne, Bruno Walter,

George Perle, and many others.

Holdings: 600,000 volumes, 400,000 pieces of sheet music, 100,000 photographs, 5,000 set and costume designs for opera, 6,000 prints of musicians' portraits, over 850 English and foreign language journals.

Services: Photocopying on premises, photo reproduction of microfilms (price varies). The Music Division's professional staff answers brief reference queries by phone during open hours at (212) 870-1650. The Music Division accepts reference questions by email and fax from persons located outside New York City. The email service is available through the web page.

Jerome Robbins Dance Division
Third Floor
(212) 870-1657
www.nypl.org/research/lpa/dan/dan.html
dance@nypl.org

Madeleine M. Nichols, Curator
Monica Mosley, Assistant Curator

Hours: 12:00 pm – 6:00 pm, Tuesday, Wednesday, Friday, Saturday
12:00 pm – 8:00 pm, Thursday

Subject Strengths: The largest and most comprehensive archive in the world devoted to the documentation of dance. The collection's 30,000+ reference books represent only three percent of its holdings; other resources are periodicals, programs, costume and scenic designs, manuscripts (primarily correspondence), posters and photographs, audio tapes of oral history, and videotapes and films. Access to the archive is provided by online catalogue and the ten-volume "Dictionary Catalog of the Dance Collection."

Special Collections: Denishawn Collection; Humphrey-Wiedman Collection; Hanya Holm Collection; Roger Pryor Dodge Collection of Nijinsky photographs; Chamie Collection of Ballet Russe materials; Fania Marinoff Collection of 3,500 photographs by Carl van Vechten; Walter Owen Collection; Cia Fornaroli Collection of 19th-Century Itralian Dance; Isadora Duncan Collection; Astruc-Diaghilev Collection; Ruth Page Collection; Lincoln Kirstein Collection; Lillian Moore Collection; Rouben Ter-Arutunian Collection. Also gifts from the estates of Agnes de Mille, Angna Enters, Jose Limon, Pauline Lawrence Limon, Walter Terry,

Sol Hurok, George Platt Lynes, Irving Deakin, Jose Greco, Alexandra Danilova. New York City Ballet, American Ballet Theatre, Dance Theatre of Harlem, Joffrey Ballet, and Brooklyn Academy of Music. AIDS Oral History Project focuses on the lives and work of dance professionals who are at risk due to HIV and AIDS and adds to the Oral History Project begun in 1974 to more fully document the work of Frederick Ashton, George Balanchine, Martha Graham, Leonid Massine, Alexandra Danilova, Alicia Markova, Ninette de Valois, and Lucia Chase.

Services: Photocopying on premises, photo reproduction of items, telephone reference service. Films and videos are available on a first-come, first-served basis. Some films require written permission from the donor before they can be viewed (call for information).

The Rodgers and Hammerstein Archives of Recorded Sound
Third Floor
(212) 870-1663
Fax: (212) 870-1720
www.nypl.org/research/pa/rha/rha.html
rha@nypl.org

Don McCormick, Curator

Hours: 12:00 pm – 6:00 pm, Tuesday, Wednesday, Friday, Saturday
12:00 pm – 8:00 pm, Thursday

Subject Strengths: Recorded literature and speech, video tapes and films (opera and music performances, rock videos, master classes, and public television broadcasts), and printed materials covering the entire field of sound recording. Among the theatre figures are recordings of Bert Williams, Paul Robeson, P. T. Barnum, and Tennessee Williams.

Special Collections: Trinity Repertory Theatre Oral History; New York Shakespeare Festival/Public Theater Collection of Sound Recordings; Benedict Stambler Memorial Archive, Jewish music and theatre; Toscanini legacy; WNEW, popular music 1930-1960; Favorite Story, literary works adapted by Jerome Lawrence and Robert E. Lee for radio (1940s); Metropolitan Opera Broadcasts (1930-present); Society for Asian Music; Heritage of the March; Bell Telephone Hour; Marian McPartland Piano Jazz. Personal collections of soprano Rosa Ponselle; pianist and conductor Rosalyn Tureck; composers Richard Rodgers, Deems Taylor, John Watts,

Paul Jacobs, Joseph Schillinger; conductor Thomas Scherman; Yiddish artist Ruth Rubin; singers Lanny Ross and Libby Holman; and many others. William Wolf Film & Theater Interview Collection, 1972-1998.

Holdings: The archive contains approximately 600,000 recordings and 12,000 printed items.

Services: Photocopying on premises, photo reproduction of items, telephone reference service. Researchers may listen to recordings at stations in the archive, and, depending on copyright law interpretation, have copies made for a fee.

Billy Rose Theatre Collection
Third Floor
(212) 870-1639
Fax: (212) 870-1868
www.nypl.org/research/lpa/the/the.html
theatrediv@nypl.org

Bob Taylor, Librarian

Hours: 12:00 pm – 6:00 pm, Tuesday, Wednesday, Friday, Saturday
12:00 pm – 8:00 pm, Thursday

Subject Strengths: Formally established in 1931 from a bequest of David Belasco, the collection contains approximately 5 million items. The archive's roots actually date to two other important gifts—the George Becks Collection of 18th and 19th century scripts and promptbooks, and the Robinson Locke Collection of scrapbooks from 1970 to 1920. Printed materials range from standard reference books and biographies to 19th century magic manuals, from early trade journals to current fan magazines and scholarly journals. Scripts and promptbooks date from the early 19th century to the present. The collection also includes millions of programs, thousands of set, costume and lighting designs, clipping files, personal archives and scrapbooks, prints, photographs, and posters. The Theatre on Film and Tape Archive (TOFT) houses hundreds of film and video recordings of theatre performances, documentaries, and award shows. Books and periodicals published since 1972 can be found catalogued in the online catalogue CATNYP. Materials published before 1972 may be located in the free-standing card catalogue, or Parts I and II of the "Dictionary-Catalogue of the Theatre and Drama Collections, Part III: Non-Book Collection."

Special Collections: Hiram Stead Collection (British theatre, 1709-1932); Alex Gard and Al Frueh Collection (caricatures); Henin Collection (French theatre, 1600-1900); Edward Harrigan Collection (manuscripts); Samuel Ellison Collection (magic and waxworks); Liebler Collection; Hallie Flanagan Davis Collection; Francis Bruguiere Collection (Neighborhood Playhouse, Provincetown Playhouse, and Theatre Guild); Chamberlin and Lyman Brown Theatrical Agency Collection; design collections of Claude Bragdon, Nat Karson, Aline Bernstein, Donald Oenslager, Lee Simonson, Howard Bay, Jo Mielziner, Boris Aronson, and Jules Fischer; photographic collections of Carl van Vechten and the Vandamm and White studios; press materials in the George Kleine and Winthrop Ames Collection; and collections of major film studios including Paramount, Universal, MGM and the Motion Picture Producers and Distributors of America Collection. Personal papers of directors such as A. J. Antoon and Harold Clurman; authors such as Clifford Odets, Michael Stewart, John Van Druten, and Betty Comden and Adolph Green; producers such as Cheryl Crawford, Maurice Evans, and Harold Prince; and performers such as Montgomery Clift and Gypsy Rose Lee.

Services: Photocopying on premises, photo reproduction of items, telephone reference service. Advanced appointments are necessary to view materials in the TOFT Archive; call (212) 870-1642. The Theatre Collection accepts reference questions by email and fax from persons located outside New York City. Supply your full name and mailing address.

Schomburg Center for Research in Black Culture
515 Malcolm X Boulevard
New York, NY 10037
(212) 491-2200
http://www.nypl.org/research/sc/sc.html

General Research and Reference Division
Phone: 212 491 2218
scgrrref@nypl.org
Genette McLaurin, Associate Chief Librarian

Hours: 12:00 pm - 8:00 pm, Tuesday and Wednesday
12:00 pm - 6:00 pm, Thursday and Friday
10:00 am - 6:00 pm, Saturday

Holdings: The general reference department holds clipping files, scripts, books, and period scrapbooks; books and periodicals

51

related to Africa, American theatre, and performance. Also included are materials on performance in Africa and the Caribbean.

Manuscripts, Archives, and Rare Books Division
Manuscripts, Archives, and Rare Books Division
(212) 491-2224
Fax: (212) 491-2037
www.nypl.org/research/sc/scm/marb.html
scmarbref@nypl.org

Diana Lachatanere, Curator

Hours: 12:00 pm - 5:00 pm, Wednesday and Thursday
10:00 am - 5:00 pm, Friday and Saturday

Holdings: The collection contains materials that document the history and culture of peoples of African descent throughout the world, with a concentration on the Americas and the Caribbean. Subject emphasis includes the performing and visual arts. The broadsides, programs, and playbills collections primarily document theatrical, cultural, social, and political events in the United States from the late 19th century to the present. The sheet music collection contains spirituals, folk songs, ragtime, blues, jazz, gospel, popular songs, show tunes and European classical music by composers of African descent. The collection also features personal papers and theatrical records (The Helen Armstead-Johnson Collection, the Negro Ensemble Company, Clarence Cameron White, and Luther Henderson, among many others). Finding aids are accessible on the division's website.

Moving Image and Recorded Sound Division
Moving Image and Recorded Sound Division
(212) 491-2236
www.nypl.org/research/sc/scl/mirs.html

James Briggs Murray, Curator

Hours: 10:00 am - 5:00 pm, Tuesday to Saturday, by appointment

Holdings: Primarily a collection of documentary films, its holdings include films on Lorraine Hansberry, the Negro Ensemble Company, and Rosa Alberta, among others, as well as approximately 50 plays on film and video.

Services: Most sound recordings and videos are played through a remote playback system to patrons in semi-private listening/viewing facilities; no appointment is generally required for access to these materials. Motion picture films, however, are shown only on scanners (for preservation reasons) and are shown by appointment only.

Photographs and Prints Department
(212) 491-2201

www.nypl.org/research/sc/scg/photo.html
scphotoref@nypl.org

Mary Yearwood, Curator

Hours: 12:00 pm - 5:00 pm, Wednesday to Friday
10:00 am - 5:00 pm, Saturday

Subject Holdings: Included in the 300,000 images is a large collection of photographs related to African- American theatre and dance.

Subject Holdings: Included in the 300,000 images is a large collection of photographs related to African-American theatre and dance.

New York Society Library
53 East 79th Street
New York, NY 10021
(212) 288-6900
www.nysocilib.org

Hours: 9:00 am – 5:00 pm, Monday, Wednesday, Friday, Saturday
9:00 am - 7:00 pm, Tuesday and Thursday
1:00 pm – 5:00 pm, Sunday
Closed weekends during the summer

Holdings: The library contains over 2,500 biographies, many of which are related to theatre and performance. It also houses a substantial number of early editions of American and English plays.

Services: As the Society Library is a subscription library, books are available for circulation only to those who subscribe (basic membership $200/year). The library does allow non-members to review materials on-site in the first-floor reading room.

New York Times Archive

Access to the corporate archives is limited to *Times* employees only.

New York University
Elmer Holmes Bobst Library
70 Washington Square South
New York, NY 10012-1091
(212) 998-2500
Fax: (212) 995-4829
www.nyu.edu/library/bobst

Peter Jaffe, Supervisor for Circulation and Library Privileges
peter.jaffe@nyu.edu

Pamela Bloom, Theater and Performing Arts Librarian
pamela.bloom@nyu.edu
(212) 998-2618

Hours: 7:00 am – midnight, seven days a week

Holdings: Circulating collection includes 2.5 million volumes, 2.3 million microforms, periodicals, and other materials.

Services: A Library Metro Card is required for access to the general collection. Outside researchers may present their Library Metro Card at the library Monday to Thursday 9:00 am – 10:45 pm, Friday 9:00 am – 6:45 pm, Saturday 10:00 am – 6:45 pm, and Sunday 1:00 pm – 9:45 pm.

Fales Collection
Third Floor
(212) 988-2596
Fax: (212) 995-3835
www.nyu.edu/library/bobst/research/fales
fales.library@nyu.edu

Hours: 10:00 am – 6:00 pm, Monday to Thursday
　　　　9:00 am – 5:00 pm, Friday

Holdings: The Fales Library, comprising nearly 200,000 volumes and 7,000 linear feet of archive and manuscript materials, houses both the Fales Collection of rare books and manuscripts in English and American literature, the Downtown Collection, the Food and Cookery Collection, and general special collections from the NYU libraries. Collection descriptions and finding aids are available at www.nyu.edu/library/bobst/research/fales/cdfa.htm.

Special Collections: The Downtown Collection documents East Village and SoHo artistic and literary culture from 1974 to the mid 1990s. Collection highlights include the David Wojnarowicz Papers, the Mark Hall Amitin/World of Culture for the Performing Arts, Inc. Archive, and the Judson Memorial Church Archive, which includes material on the Judson Dance Theater, Judson Poets Theater, and Judson Gallery. Recent acquisitions include the Mabou Mines Archive, 1970-1995, the Richard Foreman Papers, and the Richard Hell Papers, 1969-2003.

Services: The Fales Library operates on a closed stack system and Fales/Special Collection items do not circulate. Patrons may bring laptops into the reading room. Appointments are necessary to consult manuscript and archival materials.

Tamiment Library/Robert F. Wagner Labor Archives
Bobst Library, Tenth Floor
70 Washington Square South
New York, NY 10012
Tel: (212) 998-2630
Fax: (212) 995-4225
www.nyu.edu/library/bobst/research/tam

Dr. Michael Nash, Head
michael.nash@nyu.edu

Hours: 10:00 am – 5:45 pm, Monday to Friday
          10:00 am - 5:00 pm, most Saturdays during the academic year
          Summer Hours: 10:00 am - 5:00 pm, Monday to Thursday; Fridays by prior appointment only; closed Saturdays

Subject Strengths: One of the nation's oldest and largest repositories for materials dealing with labor and radical movements. Among its theatre-related holdings are records of Actors' Equity Association, Associated Actors and Artists (The Four A's), and American Guild of Musical Artists, IATSE, NABET, AFTRA, the

Actors' Fund, the Labor Theater, and the Tamiment Playhouse.

Holdings: The collections include photographs, oral history interviews, and rare publications dealing with labor and radical theater history. Brief descriptions of archival collections can be found in BobCat, NYU Library's online catalog (www.bobcat.nyu.edu), and detailed guides to some individual collections are available on the Tamiment Library's website.

Services: The Tamiment Library is open to the public; visitors unaffiliated with NYU or its consortium partners should request a day pass to visit the collections at the Library Privileges desk in the lobby of Bobst Library. Once at the Tamiment Library researchers must register to use the collections and obtain a Tamiment Library card valid for one year.

P.S. 122

150 First Avenue
New York, NY 10009
(212) 477-5829
Fax: (212) 353-1315
www.ps122.org
ps122@ps122.org

Anne Dennin, Executive Director

Holdings: The materials are not organized, but do include clippings, programs, posters, and videotapes.

PARSONS SCHOOL OF DESIGN

Adam and Sophie Gimbel Design Library
2 West 13th Street, 2nd Floor
New York, NY 10011
(212) 229-8914
Fax: (212) 229-2806
www.newschool.edu/library/gimbel

Amy Schofield, Acting Director

Hours: 8:00 am – 8:45 pm, Monday to Thursday
8:00 am – 5:45 pm, Friday
12:00 pm – 6:00 pm, Saturday
12:00 pm – 8:00 pm, Sunday

Holdings: The collection focuses most strongly on those subject areas for which Parsons has departments: architecture and environmental design, fashion design, fine arts, illustration, interior design, lighting design, painting, photography, product design, and sculpture. The Picture Collection contains approximately 50,000 pictures and reproductions culled from a variety of publications. The Kellen Archives Center is a repository for archival materials relating to the history of art and design, with a special focus on the history of the school and the careers of its faculty, students, alumni, and other associates.

JÓZEF PIŁSUDSKI INSTITUTE OF AMERICA FOR RESEARCH IN THE MODERN HISTORY OF POLAND

180 Second Avenue
New York, NY 10003
(212) 505-9077
Fax: (212) 505-9052
www.pilsudski.org/English/Collections/Archives.html
info@pilsudski.org

Iwona Korga, Vice Director of the Józef Piłsudski Institute

Hours: 10:00 am – 5:00 pm, Monday to Friday

Special Collections: Documentary and historical films.

Holdings: The library features more than 22,000 volumes, primarily related to the modern history of Poland. The collection has slim holdings in theatre consisting of actors' memoirs and Bogoslawski texts on acting and theatre history (mostly in Polish).

PLAYBILL, INC.

525 Fashion Avenue, Room 1801
New York, NY 10018
(212) 557-5757
www.playbill.com

Louis Botto, Senior Editor

Holdings: Playbill does not have research facilities. Currently the company has only one copy of each playbill, as holdings from 1924-1992 were sold to the Harvard Theatre Collection (pre-1924 holdings were destroyed by a fire).

QUEENS COLLEGE (CUNY)

Rood-Scanlan Theatre Collection
Benjamin Rosenthal Library
65-30 Kissena Boulevard
Flushing, NY 11367
(718) 997-3700
www.qc.edu

Richard Wall, Drama, Theatre, and Dance Bibliographer
rlw$lib@qc1.qc.edu

Hours: By appointment only

Holdings: 8,500 books; 20,000 microforms; 100 periodicals;
20,000 programs; 400 posters; 150 scrapbooks; 6,000 clipping
files; 5,000 photographs; 250 play scripts, screenplays, and
libretti; 500 disc recordings; plus set designs and blueprints. A
substantial amount of the collection is in storage and is not catalogued.

Subject Strengths: Emphasis is heaviest in the areas of late
19th- and early 20th-century American theatre (pre-1940) with
British theatre, world cinema, and dance also represented. Also
includes rare material on regional theatre at the turn of the
century.

Special Collections: Donors include Arnold Rood (Queens
College alumnus); Lester Sweyd, theatrical agent; and the George
P. Montgomery scrapbooks, a twelve-volume indexed
collection of ephemera.

QUEENS HISTORICAL SOCIETY

The Kingsland Homestead
143-35 37th Avenue
Flushing, NY 11354
(718) 939-0647, ext. 15
Fax: (718) 539-9885
www.queenshistoricalsociety.org
info@queenshistoricalsociety.org

Richard Hourahan, Collections Manager

Hours: 10:00 am – 5:00 pm, Tuesday and Thursday, by appointment

Holdings: The collection includes libretti from the Metropolitan Opera in Italian, French, or German with English translations, dating from 1920-1970. The archive has 86 theatre drawings and also over 90 theatre programs, including such Broadway hits as *The Glass Menagerie, A Streetcar Named Desire, Oklahoma!,* and *South Pacific.* Miller Sisters Collection (photos from birth to death, including minor stardom on Broadway).

Services: After the first hour of research, fees apply ($15/hour).

QUEENS PUBLIC LIBRARY
89-11 Merrick Boulevard
Jamaica, NY 11432
(718) 990-0755
Fax: (718) 658-8342
www.queenslibrary.org
elee@queenslibrary.org

Hours: 10:00 am – 9:00 pm, Monday to Friday
10:00 am – 5:30 pm, Saturday
12:00 pm – 5:00 pm, Sunday (mid-September to May)

Holdings: The theatre collection has a large assortment of reference materials, as well as plays and videos (in the Literature and Language Division), history books, CDs, cassettes, and scores to musicals.

Long Island Division
(718) 990-0770
Fax: (718) 658-8342 (attn: Judith Box)
www.queenslibrary.org/central/longisland

Judith Box, Division Manager
judith.box@queenslibrary.org

Hours: 10:00 am – 9:00 pm, Monday
10:00 am – 7:00 pm, Tuesday to Thursday
10:00 am – 6:00 pm, Friday
10:00 am – 5:30 pm, Saturday
12:00 pm – 5:00 pm, Sunday (mid-September to May)

Holdings: The Long Island Division collects materials related to life in Brooklyn, Queens, and Long Island. Materials are catalogued geographically, and include some theatre programs, photographs, and clippings. More information on film and cinema is available, including materials on the Astoria Studios.

RADIO CITY MUSIC HALL

Corporate Library and Archives
(212) 965-0094
Fax: (212) 965-0419
www.radiocity.com

Holdings: Covering performance at the music hall since its opening in 1932, materials include programs, photographs, posters, slides, films and videos, clippings, sheet music, costume and set designs, and promotional merchandise.

Services: Hours are limited. The library and archives are primarily for corporate use, but the archivist will assist with scholarly inquires via phone and fax.

ROUNDABOUT THEATRE COMPANY

231 West 39th Street, Suite 1200
New York, NY 10018
(212) 719-9393
Fax: (212) 869-8817
www.roundabouttheatre.org
info@roundabouttheatre.org

Holdings: Archive materials cover productions at the Roundabout since 1966 and include production notes, reviews, playbills, promptbooks, design sketches, and magazines.

SHUBERT ARCHIVE

149 West 45th Street
New York, NY 10036
(212) 944-3895
Fax: (212) 944-4139
www.shubertarchive.org
information@shubertarchive.org

Maryanne Chach, Archivist

Hours: 10:00 am – 5:00 pm, Monday to Friday, by application and appointment only. For an application, visit the web site or request one by phone or fax.

Subject Strengths: Business and artistic records in the archive cover every aspect of the Shuberts' careers as producers and managers. The earlier documents date from the 1890s; the majority covers the first three decades of the 20th century.

Special Collections: Correspondence (1900-1970): general office and business correspondence, some personal papers. Legal & Financial Records (1900-1979): contracts and booking arrangements, theatre and production management records, box office statements, real estate negotiations, corporate records, ledgers and journals, financial transactions, and documents concerning legal actions. Music (1900-1940): manuscript and published scores and sheet music, including materials acquired in London, Berlin, Vienna, Paris, and Budapest. Scripts (1900-): English and foreign language transcripts, translations into English from French and German, revue sketches, lyrics, and synopses. Costume Designs (1900-1940): 3,000 items, mostly from the 1920s. Technical Drawings (1900-1960): includes some set designs, mostly from the 1920s. Architectural Plans (1900-1970): theatre and commercial properties nationwide, mainly 1910-1929, and in New York, Boston, Chicago, Philadelphia. Press and Publicity Material (1900-): clippings, programs, photographs, and posters for 3,500 shows and 2,000 theatre personalities; and Klaw and Erlanger Papers (approximately 1900-1919): mostly booking records, unprocessed.

THE SPANISH INSTITUTE

684 Park Avenue
New York, NY 10021
(212) 628-0420
Fax: (212) 734-4177
www.spanishinstitute.org

Holdings: Materials on performance in Spain, including history books and current periodicals, are available. All materials are in Spanish and do not circulate.

Services: Call ahead for an appointment, which can be arranged by the receptionist.

THEATER FOR THE NEW CITY

155 First Avenue
New York, NY 10003
(212) 254-1109
Fax: (212) 979-6570
www.theaterforthenewcity.net
info@theaterforthenewcity.net

Crystal Field, Director
crystal@theaterforthenewcity.net

Hours: By appointment only.

Holdings: Materials cover productions on the Lower East Side and in all five boroughs since the early 1970s. Files are not organized, and consist primarily of scripts, photos, and programs. Researchers are advised to submit a proposal to assist theatre personnel in processing requests for providing access to materials.

Services: Contact Crystal Field directly via phone or email to gain access.

THEATRE COMMUNICATIONS GROUP
520 Eighth Avenue, 24th Floor
New York, NY 10018-4156
(212) 609-5900
Fax: (212) 609-5901
www.tcg.org
tcg@tcg.org

Chris Shuff, Director of Managment Programs

Hours: 10:00 am – 6:00 pm, Monday to Friday

Holdings: TCG does not operate a library or archive, but can make available research it has conducted (e.g. surveys of non-profits, economic statistics, etc.). For more information on TCG and its programs, please visit the website at www.tcg.org.

UKRAINIAN ACADEMY OF ARTS AND SCIENCES
206 West 100th Street
New York, NY 10025
(212) 222-1866
Fax: (212) 864-3977
www.uvan.org

Mrs. Efremov, Librarian

Hours: By appointment only

Subject Strengths: The most extensive archive of Ukrainian history and culture outside of Ukraine, featuring 55,000 volumes and 500,000 archival items. Materials on Ukrainian performance include histories, monographs on performers and directors, and periodicals. The collection also maintains clipping files. The majority of material is in Ukrainian.

Kurt Weill Foundation for Music

Weill-Lenya Research Center
7 East 20th Street
New York, NY 10003-1106
(212) 505-5240
www.kwf.org
wlrc@kwf.org

Dave Stein, Archivist

Hours: 10:00 am – 5:00 pm, Monday to Friday, by appointment only (at least one day in advance)

Subject Holdings: The collection comprises printed music, music manuscripts, performance materials, scripts, correspondence, audio and video recordings, films, programs, posters, press clippings, business records, and the libraries of Kurt Weill and Lotte Lenya. In addition to acquiring primary research materials, the center has compiled a broad collection of published materials including scripts, dissertations, and books on music and theatre criticism, analysis, and biography. The Oral History Program includes recorded interviews with friends, collaborators, and professional associates.

Robert Wilson Archive

Byrd Hoffman Water Mill Foundation
155 Wooster Street, Suite 4F
New York, NY
(212) 253-7485
www.robertwilson.com
archive@robertwilson.com

Jason Loeffler, Archivist

Hours: By appointment only

Holdings: The Byrd Hoffman Water Mill Foundation maintains the Robert Wilson Archive, a collection of photographs, programs, press clippings, videotapes, drawings, and other documents.

Services: The collection is open to the public, but by appointment only. A donation of $25 per research day is suggested. For a detailed list of materials available consult www.robertwilson.com/works/workmaster.htm.

YIVO Institute for Jewish Research

15 West 16th Street
New York, NY 10011-6301
(212) 246-6080
Fax: (212) 292-1892
www.yivoinstitute.org/archlib/archlib_fr.html

Fuma Mohrer, Chief Archivist (fmohrer@yivo.cjh.org)
Brad Hill, Dean of the Library (bhill@yivo.cjh.org)
Aviva E. Astrinsky, Head Librarian (avastrinsky@yivo.cjh.org)

Hours:
> Library: 9:30 am – 5:30 pm, Monday to Thursday
> Archives: By appointment only

Subject Strengths: The materials in the collection concern all phases of life in Jewry in Eastern European countries and other countries in which Eastern European Jews reside. Theatre holdings include comprehensive coverage of Yiddish drama and theatre, ranging from folk plays in the Middle Ages to performances in the ghettos during the Nazi regime. Materials in the archives include scripts, playbills, programs, posters, photographs, artifacts, clippings of theatre reviews, and published and unpublished music for the Yiddish theatre.

Special Collections: Papers of prominent personalities include those of Sholem Perelmuer, Mendle Elkin, Maurice Schwartz, Abraham Goldfaden, Jacob Gordin, Mark Schweid, Boris Tomashevski, and Jacob Adler. Also available are records of the Union of Jewish Actors in Poland; the Vilna YIVO collection of posters, playbills, and photographs; and a music collection.

Services: A guide to the collections can be accessed at the YIVO web site (see URL above). In 2004, the Center for Jewish History OPAC (On Line Public Access Catalog) will feature YIVO archives and library collections. The YIVO Library does not require appointments. Archives appointments may be made by calling (212) 294-6143 or emailing archives@yivo.cjh.org.